Book 1

INVASION

The Dutch in Wartime
Survivors Remember

Edited by

Tom Bijvoet

Mokeham Publishing Inc.

Wasylyshko

© 2011 Mokeham Publishing Inc.
Box 20203, Penticton, B.C., V2A 8M1, Canada
PO Box 2090, Oroville, WA, 98844, USA
www.mokeham.com

Cover photograph by Ilya de Milde

ISBN 978-0-9868308-0-8

Contents

On the front cover

'Destroyed City', is the defining memorial sculpture commemorating the bombing of Rotterdam of May 14, 1940. The contorted figure, hands stretched up to the sky in pain, panic, desperation and possibly hope has a hole in its torso, representing the ripped-out heart of the city. The sculpture was erected on Plein 1940 (1940 Square) in Rotterdam in 1953. It was made by Osip Zadkine, a Franco-Belarussian sculptor and lithographer.

Introduction

Tom Bijvoet

In the spring of 2010, in the run up to the 65th anniversary of the liberation of The Netherlands from Nazi occupation on May 5, 1945, I started to spontaneously receive written stories about the war in The Netherlands from readers of 'Maandblad de Krant', the Dutch language magazine for immigrants to Canada and the USA that I edit. "Publish these," the authors said, "we are the last people who can pass on these important stories."

So I decided to print them - in Dutch - because they are valuable stories which contain powerful lessons about a horrific past, that one day may have to be relived if the memories are not kept alive.

Then came the requests to print these stories in English, to ensure that the Canadian and American children and grandchildren of the older immigrants, who had written these stories, would be able to read them. "Okay," I said, "we can do that, I heard these stories during my youth, I think they were formative and helped me understand how fortunate I am to have been born where I was, when I was. However, I can only do that with your help. If we do this, I need enough stories to fill a separate 28 page English language commemorative issue of the paper. So please, send me your memories!"

Sometimes you have to be careful what you ask for. I expected to have to scramble to fill the 28 pages. I need not have worried, I received more than 200 submissions with personal memories of World War II in The Netherlands and the Dutch East Indies. The problem I faced was how to select representative memories from all those stories. All the experiences were unique, all were worth publishing, but I did not have room for more than about one fifth of what I received. So I printed a selection and pledged to the people who submitted these memories that I would try to find a way to have all of their stories told. That resulted in plans for a series of small books, which we have called 'The Dutch in Wartime: Survivors Remember' each containing a number of the memories that I received, grouped thematically. This is the first volume in that series.

One of the reasons we received so many stories is of course that war is universal for those suffering under its consequences. Maybe the most revealing part of this project for me was the realization that there is no choice in the experience of war and oppression. Eight million people lived in The Netherlands in 1940 and of those eight million every single one was touched in one way or another. War is not an elective, once it is there, it is there for everyone. These books, by and large, are not about the heroes and the villains of the war. Stories about them are important too and many of them have been told since 1945. But in this series we focus on ordinary people, young adults, teenagers, children even, who had to live through an extraordinary time - people you can immediately identify with.

We start the series, logically enough, with the events of May 1940, when the German army invaded The Netherlands. We encounter people living a quiet life in a largely rural country that is suddenly disturbed by the sights and sounds and even the smells of war. We read of frustrated fathers trying to bring down German airplanes with rifle fire. We read of aerial battles, witnessed above the cities and towns of a hitherto peaceful nation. We particularly read of the way those days of battle ingrained themselves into the memories of the younger survivors, small children at the time: happiness because of a day off school, sadness because of a missed birthday. Everyday stories told against the backdrop of armed conflict. And then there are the stories of the real horrors of war: the loss of home and hearth, the death of neighbors, of siblings even, in brutal bombing raids, told, I wish to emphasize this again, by everyday people leading everyday lives.

In many of the stories we read an additional message: however bad the five days of war were, even though we did not know it at the time, worse, much worse was still to come. After capitulation of the Dutch army a tyrannical occupation of The Netherlands started. The occupation would last five years, memories of five years of shortages, persecution, outright atrocities, famine and eventually a much anticipated liberation will follow in the subsequent volumes of this series. Several of the personal stories started in this volume, sometimes just as brief snippets, will continue in more detail in these subsequent books.

On a final note I would like to urge readers not to forget, as we read these stories, that similar memories are being made right now, in many locations across the world. A sad reflection upon a sad state of affairs. But every story may help in its own little way to prevent some of these new memories from arising.

My thanks go out to all the contributors who took part in the project and urged me to keep these memories alive.

Map: Fortress Holland

The map above shows the area behind the strategic inundations and defense lines known as 'Fortress Holland'. It contains the major population centres and was meant to withstand invasion from the east for many months. This defense strategy did not take into account the use of paratroopers. The Grebbe Line was the most important defense line prior to reaching Fortress Holland.

Historical background

When the German army invaded The Netherlands few were prepared for the shock of the unexpected onslaught.

The Dutch Army, a conscript army that had been mobilized in August of 1939, but had not been active in the field since the Napoleonic wars some 130 years earlier, was only gradually getting ready. Rather than preparing for active combat the force had to spend its time building and strengthening defense works. Its weapons were obsolete and in many instances predated the First World War, which the country had evaded in quiet neutrality.

The Dutch Government had disregarded repeated warnings from its diplomats and secret service agents in Berlin that this time was different. The widely held conviction in government circles was that The Netherlands could once again remain neutral in the inevitable conflict between Nazi Germany and the forces of civilized freedom and liberal democracy. Austria, Czechoslovakia, Poland, Norway and Denmark had already been subject to Hitler's expansionary zeal, but still the Dutch Prime Minister refused to believe that The Netherlands would be sucked into the international conflict.

The Dutch people, conservative and loyal to Queen and Fatherland went about their business. The vast majority expected, as their leaders had told them, to escape war once again.

The invading German troops crossed the border into The Netherlands twenty minutes before sunrise on May 10, 1940, a beautiful spring day. The Dutch army resisted bravely, with the limited means at its disposal. Several defense lines were held against the Germans by the numerically much weaker Dutch. But paratroopers skipped those defense lines altogether and landed right in the middle of 'Fortress Holland' the densely populated west of the country that was supposed to be safe for a long time because of its defense with fortifications and strategic inundations.

Fighting between Dutch units and German paratroopers near The Hague, the residence of Queen Wilhelmina, was severe. On May 13 the royal family and the government fled the country by crossing the North Sea to England, to avoid falling into German hands. The unexpected flight of their leaders hit the morale of the Dutch people hard.

The Dutch Army put up more resistance than the German High Command had expected and a new tactic, a barbaric tactic of sheer terror, was employed. A large fleet of Heinkel bombers flew to the second largest city of The Netherlands, Rotterdam, and carpet-bombed the city centre. Huge fires broke out. 800 Rotterdammers lost their lives, 80,000 lost their homes. On May 15, when the Germans threatened to give the fourth largest city, Utrecht, the same treatment and to continue down the list until the Dutch surrendered, General Winkelman, the Commander in Chief, capitulated.

Hostilities had lasted five days, but the war would continue for five very long years.

No rifles and no ammunition

Harm Duursma

Before the war, after graduating from school every young man in The Netherlands was conscripted into the armed forces for two years. On the afternoon of August 28, 1939, the Dutch government mobilized everyone who had served and was still eligible for active duty and ordered them to return to their last base. The oldest of these men, conscripted in 1924, were anywhere from 35 to 40 years of age. On the 29th every man left for his respective base. It was funny to see some men wearing only parts of their uniform and others wearing ill-fitting uniforms that they had not worn for many years.

I lived in Hengelo and had to report in Rotterdam. My train stopped at every station along the way. Some men would get off to head for their base and others would get on to head towards mine. I arrived in Rotterdam about mid-afternoon. I had something to eat and was sent to The Hague afterwards on an open truck with some other men. We arrived at the barracks and stayed there overnight.

The next morning we were sent to our temporary home in a villa close to the navy staff building. Most of us conscripted men were assigned duties as telegraph operators, in administration and as chauffeurs for the officers. It was my duty to go into the neighboring village to receive food that arrived in containers and to bring it back to the navy staff building. Among other miscellaneous duties, I also served coffee to the admiral and other senior officers. Every three weeks I was given leave to go home to Hengelo to be with my wife and one-year old daughter.

On May 10, 1940 we awoke to explosions in the air and we saw airplanes in the distance, dropping bombs on our barracks and the airport in The Hague. A little later that morning I had to leave the villa and move into the office building. Mattresses were delivered and placed on the floor. These were to be our beds for the next while. We were told to remove our shoes when we went to bed, but were not allowed to get undressed. I was told that I was again assigned to serve coffee and food.

That same day I had to go into town to go to the police station to pick up a revolver. It was rumored to be very dangerous to be out on the streets because supposedly supporters of the Germans would shoot any man in military uniform.

Later that day a pilot came to the office and told the officers that he could not get back to the airbase in Den Helder and had put his badly damaged plane down on the beach in Scheveningen.

He learned that we had no rifles or ammunition and told the officers that he had a machine gun in his plane. If they could get somebody to volunteer to go with him to take it out of the plane, we could use it. I volunteered and the two of us got on a motorbike and rode to the plane. When we arrived there, we saw that the plane had been shot up again and a small fire had started. We grabbed our gas masks and filled them with water and used that to extinguish the fire.

While we were trying to remove the machine gun from the plane, we had to take cover several times because German planes were passing overhead. Finally we got the machine gun out and rode back on the motorbike. I sat on the back, holding the machine gun. When we arrived at the office, the pilot and I placed the machine gun on a little hill opposite the building, but it never got used. To prevent the Germans from obtaining vital information, we also burned maps and various classified documents that day.

After five days we received a telegram that the country had surrendered to the Germans, so we threw all our weapons into a pile. A little later an army vehicle arrived with officers who told us that it was not true that we had capitulated, so we picked up our arms again and were ready to fight, if necessary. After that they came back again and told us it was true after all and once again the weapons were thrown into a pile.

About half the enlisted men decided to leave for Scheveningen. They had heard that they could hire a spot on a fishing boat that would take them to England to escape to safety. I don't know if they ever arrived there. I did not go because my wife was still very weak after having given birth to our second daughter.

The day after, we were sent back to the barracks, where we found that many other navy men had arrived. The country was now under German occupation. In order to fill our days, we would be sent into different cities to do maintenance work on the streets, lawns, and ditches.

I was transferred to Haarlem. Returning from weekend leave one day, my train arrived shortly after ten o'clock. I had to hurry to my base, because there was a ten o'clock curfew now, after which no one was allowed out in the streets. One day when I arrived at my base I found that the German troops had moved in and I had no idea where my men had gone. I met a city policeman and asked him if he knew where the men had moved to. He suggested I had better accompany him to the police station. On the way over there two drunken German soldiers wanted to capture me. The four of us walked to the police station and the officer immediately placed me in a cell. I could hear loud voices outside my cell, but was unable to hear what was being said. The German soldiers must have left and the next morning I was escorted to a school where my men were now stationed.

Before the war started I had been employed as a glazier for a foundry company called Dickers in the city of Hengelo. It was allowed to recall workers, if they were needed. In January 1941 my wife received papers from Dickers requesting me to return to work.

Aiming for the gas tank

Lisette de Groot

On May 10, 1940, our family lived in Voorschoten, a small town not far from The Hague and Leiden, where my father was stationed in the Dutch Army.

At about 4 a.m. we were awakened by the droning of hundreds of airplanes. It was soon light, and overhead the sky looked black. Feeling overwhelmed, my father decided to take action. Dressed in his Army uniform, he stood in the middle of the street, his gun aimed at the airplanes. "If I could just hit the gas tank," he said, "there would be one airplane less." Although he tried for quite some time, he was not successful. Disappointed, he came back inside. Then we watched the first Dutch fighter plane being shot down, falling helplessly and burning to the ground. The pilot parachuted out and was later treated in a makeshift hospital down the street. I was impressed and subdued, as I saw the stretcher with the wounded man being carried inside.

We had watched it all through the small window in our front door, while the shooting was going on, without realizing that it was dangerous. We could easily have been hurt!

As the war continued, people learned how to protect themselves by going into the cellar, or a closet or bathroom. Sometimes only the bathroom walls of a house were left standing, but people would still be alive!

War as a birthday present

Caty de Graaf

On May 10, 1940 I woke up, went downstairs and to my dismay no one wished me a happy birthday. No one sang the Dutch birthday song. I am the fourteenth child out of a family with sixteen children and my six year old mind could not understand why no one was paying any attention to me on my special day. Something was definitely wrong.

I had noticed earlier, when I was playing on the swing in the attic, a small play table and two matching chairs. I went looking for my mother and asked her who the little table and chairs were for. I had never heard my mother curse before, but this day she did. She cursed and said to one of my brothers "it's this child's birthday." She told him to bring the table and chairs downstairs. They were set before me and I was told to have fun.

After breakfast my older sister took me to school. I walked beside her, proudly holding the jar of candies, which I would hand out to my classmates, while they would sing to me, as is the Dutch birthday custom. But when we arrived there, the school was closed. So we returned home. On our way back home we stopped at an acquaintance's house and I offered her my birthday candy. She said: "No thank you. Just go home and have a nice day!"

A confusing day

Riekje Brandsma

I had celebrated my seventh birthday on April 24, 1940 and had been going to school since April 1st. I had to take a little ferry across the canal, with the other kids and then we had to go through the fields to get to school. On May 10 we had only gone about half way when we encountered the first group returning from school. They said that the teachers stood crying outside in the school yard, that war had broken out and that German soldiers with horses were in the streets.

So we returned to our hamlet of Rohel in the south of Friesland and when we got home all the neighbors and the employees of my father's shipyard stood on the bank of the canal looking at a distant bridge where they could see Germans crossing the water. Yes, that was a confusing day.

Rifles in the kitchen

Maria Neijmeijer

May 10, 1940 was a shocking day for me in Abcoude, just south of Amsterdam. I just had my seventh birthday and at school I heard that The Netherlands were at war with Germany. I ran home. Our farm was close to my school and when I came into the kitchen, where my mother was, I saw rifles in the corner. I grabbed my mother and started to cry.

I heard voices and felt a hand on my head and someone said: "Nicht schreien, nicht schreien, don't cry, I am not going to shoot you." German soldiers had to stay at our farm. They were nice men and had been forced to fight. In the evening they were all in our living room and on the empty chairs the soldiers put photographs of their wives. They had children our age and they played with us in the cow barn.

At school I heard about German enemies and at home they were friendly men. It was a very confusing time.

One big German convoy

Gerrit Top

I was born in August of 1932, the third of four boys, on a small farm a mile and a half from Nijkerk and five miles from Putten. On May 10 as Holland was invaded by the Germans we set out to walk to Nijkerk to school as usual. I can still picture our elderly neighbor in her traditional local costume calling us to say: "Boys, I think you might as well go home. I do not think there will be school today, the Germans have invaded us."

The north-south highway, which was maybe 400 yards from where we lived was one big German convoy. Fighting went on between the Dutch and the Germans. The downtown of Nijkerk lay in ruins, a few Dutch soldiers lost their lives. There was no chance of standing up against the Reich and our beloved royal family sought their safety in England, from where they kept encouraging the Dutch to resist the occupation by the Germans.

Our first plane

Peter Verhesen

On May 10, 1940, around eight o'clock in the morning my younger sister Ann and I walked from home to school in the town of Haarle, a distance of about half a mile. I was ten years old. It was some time before we could cross the main road between Hengelo and Zwolle, because a convoy of German army trucks drove by. We looked in amazement at those green vehicles filled with helmeted men in green uniforms holding rifles between their legs. We walked on and met a farmer along the way. He had just placed his milk cans by the side of the road, for pickup by the 'milk rider'. He had two preschool-aged children with him.

I still remember what he said to us: "This will change the world. It will not affect me, but I feel sorry for my children here."

Some miles away we saw a plane circle the hill just outside Haarle, where the Palthe family, rich industrialists, had their 'castle' as we called it. It was the first time in our lives that Ann and I saw a plane. When we got to school, the teacher informed us that classes had been cancelled. We walked back home.

Soldiers in the yard

Susan Rombeek

I lived in The Hague, was 7 years old and I'll never forget that special morning of May 10, 1940. The sky was filled with a tremendous droning sound and I saw big planes flying very low, just above the roofs of the houses, dropping their bombs.

My father drove away on his motorcycle to see what was going on around nearby Ockenburg airfield, where German soldiers were reported to be parachuting down and advancing towards The Hague. He came back to tell us that the Germans were already near 'Meer en Bos' a park on Meerdervoort Avenue, a wide street on the outskirts of the city.

When we went upstairs we could see planes fighting over the seaside resort of Scheveningen on the edge of The Hague and saw some of them being shot down.

Years later I found out that I probably witnessed a friend of my father-in-law being shot down and killed that day. My father-in-law was a navy pilot, who was shot down over Moerdijk, but he managed to kill a German pilot and he set his own plane on fire, before the Germans caught him. He was sent to a prisoner of war camp in Poland.

Dutch soldiers with guns set up in our yard, while they were taking collaborators from their homes. Everyone was in uproar. At school a friend told us that her father had been killed fighting at the Grebbe Line. It was so very sad and scary, but also exciting in a way.

The Dutch forces surrendered and a couple of days

later we had Germans occupying our street. The soldiers were from Austria and were quite friendly. They were crowding the grocery stores buying everything they could get their hands on. My father warned us not to be too friendly with the soldiers, which was difficult, because they were handing out candy to us. Dad thought the situation over and finally his verdict came: "Do not talk to them!"

Book for the youth

Jerry Meents

September 25, 1939 was my 9th birthday and the last day that I went to school with candy for all the kids in my class and another bag of candy for all the teachers in the school as was the tradition in that happy pre-war time. But happiness changed into five years of fear and pain. On May 10 I was woken up by people screaming "war, war, war," but that did not mean much to me. What scared me was to see adults so scared. When Holland surrendered five days later, people started burning books from Jewish, communist and socialist authors. Some Jewish people committed suicide, it was as if you could almost taste the fear.

There was a book called 'The Book for the Youth' with stories and games, which was published by the Socialist Party. My parents could not afford the book and I had always wanted to have it. Someone was going to burn it and I took it out of the fire. The next day my mother discovered the book and took it from me and threw it back into one of the fires.

The first edicts

Roland Krijgsman

We lived in the town of Middelharnis, on the island of Goeree-Overflakkee, about twenty miles south of Rotterdam. I was twelve years old and my father woke us at five in the morning to tell us that our country was at war with Germany. Outside we could see Heinkel bombers heading toward Rotterdam to destroy the airport there. Collaborators were rounded up and locked up in one of the schools and heavily guarded. We did not go to school.

The next day there was a battle between an old Dutch biplane and some German fighters in the sky above our town. The Dutch plane was shot down, but the pilot parachuted to safety.

Five days after the war started the first German troops arrived. They commandeered a big house near the harbor. The collaborators that had been locked up were set free and except for German planes overhead, everything was quiet in the village. About a week later the first edicts were pasted to the side of our town hall: no public gatherings of more than four people; all windows to be blacked out; strictly forbidden to listen to the BBC; all arms to be handed in to the authorities.

Water for the horses

John Keulen

On the afternoon of Saturday, May 11, German troop carriers rolled through my home town of Bakhuizen on their way to the coastal town of Stavoren. I was nine years old and stood on the street corner near our house watching the show of military might with awe: all those grim faced soldiers in gray uniforms, rifles clenched between their knees, passing by.

A few hours later cavalry units on horses arrived and dismounted in the center of town near Café Hettinga, which had a pasture and stables. These cavalry men seemed more jovial than the assault troops I had seen earlier and were probably farm boys.

My friends and I were standing around watching the Germans groom their horses when one of the soldiers handed me a bucket and said: "Wasser! Schnell!" (Water! Fast!). I wasted no time executing this order and ran next door where I knew there was an outdoor pump. As fast as my nine year old legs could carry me with a heavy pail of water in my hands, I returned to the soldier who had given me the order. He smiled and said something I could not understand, patted me on the shoulder, and gave his horse something to drink.

There were some 25 or 30 horses there. Some cavalry men made camp at neighboring farms, where they also commandeered fodder for their animals.

The following day, Sunday morning, a Dutch gunboat started shelling the port of Stavoren, about five miles from our village, where the Germans were firmly embedded. The Germans returned heavy fire, and the gunboat withdrew. There were some casualties ashore. The Germans were not sure if the Dutch would launch a counter attack from IJssel Lake, and they mounted some heavy machine guns on rooftops in Bakhuizen.

The shelling continued for a while, and our family took shelter in the basement, the lowest and safest part of the house. The loud booms were the first sounds of war I heard in my young life. It was terrifying. Soon it was quiet again, and we ventured outside.

The German Army continued their advance, and moved on to capture the rest of The Netherlands. They met heavy resistance at the head of the long dike that spans IJssel Lake. They were mowed off the dike by the guns of a Dutch fort on the dike.

After only four days it was over. Little did we realize that it would be five long years before the German occupation would end, five of the most unforgettable years of our lives. It was to be a time of great sacrifice, persecution, danger, deprivation, cold winters, lack of almost everything, but for a young child, also exciting. My memories of the war are more vivid than those of any other period in my life.

Stupid grins

John Vandermeer

It was May 1940 and I was a little trouble maker of nearly nine years old. My mother had a store called 'Bensdorp' that sold chocolates, my father played the French horn in the Groningen Symphony Orchestra.

Suddenly, in the early morning of May 10, we were woken up by planes in the air shooting at each other. Then there was a tremendous bang that shook our house. A plane had crashed on top of a row of houses very near to where we lived. Of course none of the people who had streamed outside to see the spectacle in the air had ever seen anything like this.

When morning came we somehow heard that the Germans were in downtown Groningen and we had to see that of course. The city's central square was filled to the brim with Germans on motorbikes and trucks. What I remember most was the stupid grins on their faces. I wanted to hit them to remove that grin. Fortunately, my father kept me in check.

The Germans behaved very well and were under strict orders to do so in those early days. They doubled the wages for musicians and artists, which was greatly welcomed, and quite necessary as well. My mother's store had many Germans coming in to buy chocolates by the box full which they sent to their families in Germany. A German walked out of one of the neighboring stores without paying. The owner went to the place where they were stationed and the commandant got our neighbor to identify the culprit. Discipline was very strict and the man was shot. Our neighbor was very upset. He said that if he would have known, he would not have reported the man.

How the fishmonger lost his head

Adriana Meershoek-Dekkers's story, as put on paper by her husband Ernest.

The Luftwaffe planes drew wide circles in the sky. There were little cones hanging from their bellies. It was Friday, May 10, 1940, 3.45 p.m., two days before Pentecost in the small farming community of Etten in the southern province of Brabant. The children had been sent home from school early.

Just across from the Protestant church, which was used by the local air-defense volunteers as a look-out post, women were crowded around the cart of the fishmonger who was doing brisk business this Friday, a day on which the overwhelmingly Roman Catholic population of Brabant traditionally ate fish and not meat. Among the women was my mother, chatting away with her neighbors, one of whom was trying to hush her four children. My mother, Petronella, had just bought a piece of cod for the evening meal and a couple of herrings for my father, Wout Dekkers. As captain of the air-defense group, he was on the church tower, binoculars in hand, watching the planes overhead.

My oldest brother, Wim, sixteen years old, was coming up the street with horse and wagon, while my older sister, Marie, fourteen, was at home keeping an eye on my one-year old sister Nellie, the baby of the family, while cleaning the windows of our modest home. After all, it was Friday and as 'clean' Dutchmen, we had to have our premises spic-and-span for the weekend. My younger brother, Kees, eleven, was in the center of town on the steps of city hall, next to the Protestant church. He was trying to read and memorize the strange license plates of the many cars and trucks coming down the main road from the east, all escaping the onslaught of the German invasion by travelling west through the center of the village on the way to Roosendaal and the province of Zeeland. For my brother the world was full of excitement, as he had never seen so many strange vehicles. My little brother, Jan, at eight years my youngest brother, was playing in the sandbox in a neighbor's backyard with several playmates his age.

The pilots up above did not pay any attention to the people in the village. Their focus was the church steeple. The squadron leader pointed to this target and started to roll his plane. The village notary's clerk was the first to notice the aircraft and he bellowed to the gossiping women to "get indoors, because they'll throw bombs". The notary himself was standing in the doorway of his big house on the corner of the street facing the church. My mother scurried across the street to our house which was diagonally across from the notary's home. As she dashed inside, heading for the cellar to store the herrings, there was a loud bang and she heard glass shattering on the ground. Knowing that her daughter was washing the windows, she yelled: "My God, Marie, be careful! You're breaking the panes!" The house groaned and swayed and suddenly the herrings on the plate were covered in dirty dust. Dust was everywhere, and it took a moment before mother and daughter could see each other again and realized that something awful had happened.

When the first of the bombs hit, Wim's horse bolted, throwing my brother off the wagon onto the cobblestones. The horse dragged the wagon, swaying, down the road. My brother Kees, who was checking the traffic coming from the east, found himself not on the steps of city hall anymore, but right in the middle of the village park, hurting badly. He soon passed out.

The notary's house was partly gone, its office exposed and there was no sign of the front door, nor of the notary himself. They never did find his remains. All that was left of what had been a mobile fish stall just minutes before was a bloody mess. Several Belgian and French soldiers who were stationed nearby roamed about stammering "c'est terrible, terrible". The mother of the four kids lay in a grotesque bloodied heap in the middle of the road with little arms and legs strewn about her. Her husband would find her and his kids half an hour later and he literally tore out his hair at the sight of what used to be his beloved family.

The scene was utter chaos. Several women were alive, but badly maimed. Others walked about in a daze. The head of the fishmonger bobbed in a pail, together with the fish heads. It still had a smile on its lips, but its eyes showed disbelief and fear.

And the church tower? The tower was still there, untouched. It seemed that the bombs had missed their intended target entirely. Or had they? Was it by a stroke of fate that they had found other targets that ruined so many lives forever? Most likely the tower was not the main objective. The main objective might well have been to sow fear among the population and to disrupt traffic on the strategic east-west highway, which ran right through the center of the village past the city hall and the Protestant church. Whatever the case, twenty-one innocent people died in this one episode in Etten, on the very first day of war in The Netherlands.

My father quickly made his way down the steeple and started to look for his family. He found his daughters Marie and little Nellie, together with his wife all dazed, still clutching the plate of ruined herring. He found my oldest brother, Wim, and he found me as I returned from an errand at a nearby store. But he could not locate my two younger brothers. He and I scoured the village together. It did not take us long to find Jan. He was still in the sandbox, where he had been playing with the three other lads when one of the bombs fell in the yard. Only one boy survived. The bomb had killed three children instantly. One of these lads looked peaceful enough, even though the skin had been stripped from his arms and legs as if a giant potato peeler had done its job. Thankfully, he never knew what hit him. Jan had his head chopped open like a boiled egg. The whole top part of his head was cut along the front and sides and hinged only at the back. I remember seeing this and to this day I have been unable to forget. I am not sure how my father brought the sad tiding to my mother. It was very difficult to watch his grief.

That left my brother Kees, who had been watching the stream of refugees. When he woke up, he was in the local infirmary being treated by an overworked physician. Apparently, he had been hit by a piece of shrapnel that tore into his body just below the left armpit. The force of the explosion and the actual hit had catapulted him from the steps of the city hall into the center of the marketplace and he had been brought on a hand-cart to the hospital, located not far from the center of the village. He was quickly bandaged up and put to bed with dozens of other wounded. Towards morning, there was another air raid and when it was over he found himself swimming in shards of glass from the blown-out windows. He was very weak and he realized that for some reason or other he was soaking wet. When they re-examined him, they discovered that he had not only been hit by the shrapnel, but that the shrapnel had torn right through his body, narrowly missing vital organs, and that it had exited through his back, leaving a gaping untreated hole. He had been losing blood all night. Kees survived, but he still bears the ugly scars from that fateful day.

For my parents the war was not over. As if losing one child was not enough to bear, they had to give up Marie in January of 1944, after she was stricken with diphtheria. Because of the war, she was unable to get proper medical care. She was gone in fourteen days, literally bleeding to death. By then she was seventeen years old. Her classmate, who sat next to her at school and came down with the disease at the same time, survived and so did I, although I had slept in the same bed right next to her. Marie succumbed, leaving my parents devastated. Until the day he died, my father could not bear to hear, see or smell anything to do with Germany, whether it be music, a Christmas tree, or food - in fact, any product made by "those people who murdered my kids".

Chicken coop

Christina Dodenbier

On May 10 we lived in Ede and much fighting was going on at the Grebbe Line, about fifteen miles from where we lived.

Our town officials being concerned about the safety of the population told us to evacuate. That meant packing what we could hold in our two hands and leaving our homes. My parents, sister and brother and I went to the countryside and slept in a chicken coop that night. It was awful!

The next morning my dad looked at our town in the distance and noticed the steeple of the church, which was in front of our house, still standing. He said: "we are going back. I'm not staying another night in this terrible place". As children we were terrified but... we went.

When we entered the familiar streets of our town there were German soldiers everywhere. They were entering and leaving our official buildings and a very queer feeling came over me. I am sure that my parents were even more aware of the serious situation. We were no longer a free country!

We found our home as we had left it the day before and life went on again.

Coal barges

Jacoba Robertson

My family lived in Veenendaal, about midway between Arnhem and Utrecht. We first heard a drone in the air from the many airplanes. All the people from our town had to walk to Elst, on the Rhine river, about an hour's walk from Veenendaal. There we boarded coal barges. We ended up in Heemskerk, north of Haarlem, on a farm, where the farmer let us stay in the barn. After a week we were back in Veenendaal.

Whenever I see people on television that have to flee in long lines, including seniors and children, I always think: that was us, in 1940.

We had a shelter in our hallway for everyone in our street. Whenever the sirens sounded everyone had to get into the shelter, until the 'all clear signal' was given. We experienced awful times.

Seasick

Gerty Heinen

When the war started mom, dad and five kids lived in the twin town of Bunschoten-Spakenburg. At one time Bunschoten and Spakenburg were separate entities. Spakenburg was a fishing village on the south end of IJssel Lake. Bunschoten, a few miles south of Spakenburg, was an agricultural community. My mother was born in Spakenburg, my father in Bunschoten. Soon after war broke out our entire town had to be evacuated because it was directly in the firing lines of the German guns. The boats of the fishing fleet were loaded up with the town's population and mom and the kids ended up on a boat heading for Enkhuizen, a town to the northwest on the other side of IJssel Lake. In no time at all my brothers John and Frank became violently seasick. Mom sat with one boy in each arm as they kept vomiting. After arriving in Enkhuizen, the evacuees were taken in by the people of that town, who opened their homes to them. After a number of days, mom had enough of being an evacuee and she wanted to go home to reunite her family. She found our neighbor, Willem van Dijk, and asked him if there was any way to get back to Bunschoten. Eventually he found some land transportation and Mom and her children returned home. They were the first ones to get back to Bunschoten. Dad had been in hiding somewhere and soon returned home also. Mom said that no matter what would happen, she was not leaving again. So in 1944, when another evacuation took place, she stayed put.

No room for the pram

Willy Mensing Traa

I t was May and I walked the customary twenty minutes to Kindergarten in the morning, wearing my wooden shoes. When I got to school, Sister told us that we had to go home again immediately. She said we were not allowed to play on our way home, but had to go straight back. I ran all the way home, glad to have a day off school. When I got home mother stood waiting with my thirteen month old sister in her pram, my five siblings and everything we could carry.

My father had been ordered to help evacuate the cattle with the other men in the village, so my mother was on her own with all the kids. We all had to assemble in a central location, where a coal truck was waiting. When we got there it turned out that there was no room for the pram. The truck was already filled with other people from our neighborhood, but we could still fit in. The truck took us the five miles to the city of Amersfoort.

We got to Amersfoort and spent a whole day sitting on one of the platforms of the railway station. The train was not allowed to leave, because of the danger of an aerial attack. As a five year old girl I sensed the sorrow of the situation: the mothers with the crying babies, people with thermos flasks sharing their coffee.

In the evening we were finally allowed to board a train and we arrived in the village of De Rijp near Alkmaar in the middle of the night. We were brought to a church, where we got coffee and sandwiches. It was the first food we got since our breakfast before we had headed to school. It tasted so good.

In the morning my three year old brother and I were billeted with two old men. We slept together in one of those old fashioned Dutch bed-closets in the wall. That was comfy and warm.

Can you imagine how the people of that little village did their best to help all those people and to give them a roof over their heads for two weeks? That must have been quite the endeavor.

Too dreadful to imagine

Jack de Pagter

I do not know what time it was when we were awakened by explosions, but we knew they were close by. It was not even daylight when I got up. The windows were shaking and there were many explosions and bursts as if we were in the middle of a severe thunderstorm with fireworks going off. Within a few minutes we were all awake and up and looking around. We now heard planes and the explosions of bombs. The windows were chattering as if they shivered from the cold.

Everyone ran outside to see what was going on. In the dim light of morning we could see planes flying very low and we heard bombs falling in our neighborhood.

We knew within minutes that they were bombs: you could hear a whistle and then an explosion. We were all outside: our neighbors in morning robes, some in just shorts, everyone wanting to see what it was all about. I was amazed that no one got hurt. We saw planes, big ones, metal ones, and they did not even have a swastika marked on them.

We watched the sky. In no time we realized that those death boxes were German planes. Like all our neighbors standing outside and looking up at the sky, we knew that we were being attacked by Germany. We saw a big plane on fire and we could see a swastika, so we knew it was German. We were certain that the Germans were bombing us and we saw another plane coming down in flames. We screamed for joy, again a German plane was hit! Later we discovered that 134 German planes were shot down during that bombing raid.

Everyone, grown-ups, children and barking dogs were running like idiots. My brother Piet and I thought it was rather interesting and we did not want to go back in the house. We lived in the southern part of The Hague, on the last block in that town. We could see the buildings of Ypenburg Airport, not far from our house, a few more houses and two farms. We could see the German planes diving and dropping bombs on the airport. This went on until the sun came up. When we could see the planes, we would scream "Plane number forty-three!"

Then the Dutch soldiers set up anti-aircraft guns in front of our house. We boys thought it was great and we were standing right next to them, encouraging them. "Hit the bastards, hit them!" we yelled. The soldiers told us to get inside because it was too dangerous to be out there!

Mom had started breakfast but no one was hungry and everything was so confused that we did not know if we were coming or going. Piet and I had a good time running from one side of the street to the other.

The Hague had three airports: one on the east side of town, one in the west and one in the south. They were military airports built to protect The Hague, because The Hague was the seat of government. Close to us was Ypenburg, the one to the north was called Valkenburg and the third was called Ockenburg. Later on we discovered that the Germans wanted to destroy the military bases, and I am glad to say that they never got one of them.

We never gave it a second thought that we were in

danger until a neighbor lady showed us a hole in her front door where a piece of shrapnel had landed. "You see, it only missed me by centimeters!" she said. The soldiers in front of our house were still shooting at the German planes and they were pleased to report that they had gotten at least sixty!

Mom was petrified. Besides trying to help the neighbors, she was constantly calling to us: "Come inside!" Once inside, we had to stay away from the windows. Liz, our neighbor, came over to show us the piece of shrapnel that had barely missed her head. My first thought was that German planes were flying over Holland on their way to bomb England and that our government did not allow that because we were neutral. Why else would they attack us?

By now, we had turned on the radio. The programs usually started at 8.00 a.m., but they were already on the air reporting that German paratroopers were landing around the Moerdijk Bridges. More paratroopers were around The Hague and Leiden. The radio warned: "Beware of those who are helping the Germans. They are in civilian clothes and some are dressed as policemen and some as nuns!"

We were horrified. This way, we could not trust anyone. We realized we were at war and there was no one to help us. All sorts of messages were broadcast over the radio and it gave us a terrible feeling. "Paratroopers all over, beware!" they constantly said. They might enter your house and use it as an information center.

Outside they were still bombing and our soldiers were shooting at the German planes. The sirens were going constantly and it would drive you insane. We learned fast that a rapid up and down siren sound meant 'alarm' and that a long siren meant 'everything is clear'.

The bombing had stopped for a while and we dared to go outside. I had to go to school for my German exam, but thought: 'To hell with that! Why do I want to learn that language anyway? Those bandits!'

For most of that day we were glued to the radio and did not want to miss a thing. We waited until 8 a.m. and had the feeling we had been up for days. We wanted to hear the news.

The newsreader read a proclamation by the Queen. We heard that fighting was going on around Arnhem and in the province of Limburg and that paratroopers were trying to get the airfields around The Hague in order to capture the Dutch government and force it to surrender. So far they had not succeeded.

We heard that Belgium and Luxembourg were also attacked and even that small country, Luxembourg, showed resistance. Dad kept saying: "We do not allow any German to fly over our neutral country." He thought it would be over within a few hours.

Of course it did not make any difference. His words were good for our morale and there was always hope, it could be true. Then we knew for sure that we were at war with those eastern murderers. Special bulletins came over the radio and there was no doubt! Holland was at war!

After the news, I decided to get to school. I could still make it by 8.30, so I left home. The sirens had started again, but we just ignored them: a new air attack.

The school was closed but the superintendent was standing in front with all our teachers. He made a good and short but emotional speech. "We Dutch have been at war with many other countries in the world and we should not be proud of that. We fought the Vikings and the Normans for many years. We fought the British and the Spaniards for eighty years and we were occupied by the French under Napoleon for thirty-six years. Now we're being attacked by the Germans and we are sure, even if it takes years, that they will not master us." The speech was so moving that two teachers cried! He said a short prayer and we all went home. We were teenagers and had no time to be emotional.

The sirens were going again! Get Shelter! Where?! We did not have any basements, we lived below sea level. There were no cellars, only a few large houses had those. My shelter was home and that is where I went.

We lived downstairs in an apartment building and when I arrived there were so many neighbors at our house that I thought there was a special meeting going on to stop the Germans on our block. Mr. Kool, the upstairs neighbor, was so nervous that he was bleeding out of his nose and it did not want to stop. Mom was trying to fix breakfast for everybody, but the gas supply was constantly turned down, so only a little bit of gas came out of the stove. We were still not hungry anyway.

Germany's plan to conquer Holland in a matter of hours did not work. Arnhem, only twenty minutes from the German border stood strong and the enemy could not get across the big rivers. We were in The Hague, about one hundred miles from the German border, but we were protected by many big rivers and the Dutch had blown up many bridges to stop the enemy.

German paratroopers were still being dropped around bridges and big rivers. Our soldiers, and we did not have many, were still shooting at German planes. We were warned that the German sixth column had planted many spies in the Low Countries long ago and that we should be alert for people who could not speak Dutch very well. A group was formed that was allowed to stop anyone in our neighborhood and ask them to say 'Scheveningen'. Only the Dutch can pronounce that word and my brother Piet and I, with many other young men our age, signed up and volunteered immediately. Foreigners who had lived in Holland for over fifty or sixty years still could not say 'Scheveningen'. Not one Dutchman objected to a spot exam on pronunciations, and it was fun doing it. If anyone could not pronounce the word properly, we were to turn him over to a policeman or a Dutch soldier. Several were caught, but we never knew what happened to them. Some turned out to be French or English. They understood why we were doing this and never caused any difficulty.

After a few hours, I decided to go downtown. Dad had gone to work at the Navy Department, where his office was. To be honest, I did not know why I wanted to go downtown. Excitement I think: I did not want to miss anything. We were still being bombed. Unbelievable! I was walking to the center of town when a bomb hit the Bethesda Hospital. I was so close to the hospital that I thought I had been hit! I remember it clearly: There was a large warehouse and I saw the window of the showroom bulging like a big belly, but the window did not break! This cured me of wandering and I wanted to go home. The sirens were still going and wherever you were, the people called you in for shelter. Never in my life have I had such an experience: We were one nation, one people. We were never as united as during those terrifying days.

When I got home our windows were full of paper tape. The tape was glued over the glass windows from left to right and from top to bottom. The reason was that if a bomb fell close by and shattered the windows, the pieces of glass would not fly in all directions. Smart thinking! There were mattresses standing against the wall during the night to protect us from bomb splinters. I told Mom that on my way back from town I had seen a man standing in front of his house with a large kitchen knife in his hand, telling everyone that passed by that no German was going to enter his house! The German's throat would be cut with that knife.

Some people were at their limits. Many things went on that day that were not realistic, but I could certainly understand. No one knew what to do or what to say.

Dad must have stayed at work because he had not come home. I presumed that my other brothers must have gone to work also. My sister Louisa had stayed at home and was the calmest of them all. We were going to have a cup of coffee but the gas was turned off again. If the gas tank were hit, there would be a big explosion and a big fire would start and the water supply of The Hague was at its lowest because of all the fires throughout the city.

It was nice and warm outside, but since we had been up since 4.30 in the morning, I decided to take a nap. One never knew what the night might bring. I must have been out within minutes.

When I awoke, we had different soldiers in front of our house and everyone wanted to give them something to eat or drink. It made us feel good. We were protected. The radio announced that the German army had now surrounded Arnhem. The announcer told the Dutch who were already occupied and under German rule to hide all liquor, wine and beer. It was feared that the Germans might get drunk and shoot anybody who showed opposition to them. To be on the safe side that night we finished our stock of 'Boerenjongens' (raisins soaked in brandy), which was strong stuff.

We heard on the radio that the Belgians were putting up a stiff fight in the Ardennes. It must have been like it was in Holland - so many Germans against so few Dutch and Belgians.

The following day it was just plain war. We were getting used to it. We got up, knew exactly if the air was clear of planes or if we had to be alert for enemy fire. There was little gas pressure. It took a long time before the water was boiling to have a cup of tea. We did not need any electricity, except to listen to the radio.

We could hear the BBC from London, but they did not give any war bulletins, so we did not have much of an idea of what was going on in Belgium and France. The German radio in all occupied countries announced that the Reich was winning on all fronts. That was to become a standard propaganda statement that we would hear for the rest of the war. What could we believe? Rumors and more rumors, that's what we lived on. What a day we had had, starting so early. It felt like ages! So many things had happened.

We were told not to turn on any light that would shine outside that evening. We had our first curfew in many years. It did not bother us very much because the sun would go down at about 8.30 or a quarter to nine, as we were on daylight savings time.

Our neighbor, Mr. Kool, the one with the severe nose bleed, turned very religious and started to preach to everyone who was around.

I do not remember what we ate or what time it was, but we decided to go to bed with our mattresses leaned up against the windows. We all slept so well that none of us heard a sound during the night. The people were so exhausted that they didn't care anymore. Everyone was so tired.

The schools were closed and, being a student, I was always thinking of going to school. Once in a while I was thinking of studies, but the events of those first days of war kept me so occupied that I was more concerned with staying alive than with my study books. If we only knew what was going on in the world! What would America think? The Dutch East and West Indies? What would Canada think? And South Africa? We spoke the same language!

The weather was still very nice and enjoyable. A few days went by, there was no news, nothing and I was astonished that you could get used to a 'war situation'.

We heard that French troops had entered the province of Zeeland where we were all born and where our grandma lived. Our hopes went up again, although we did not know what was going on. At least now we were not alone. The French were helping us.

From the German border to the Dutch coast at the North Sea was less than one hundred and ten miles. We had figured that the Germans had only moved twenty five miles. The enemy was discouraged and found out that we had flooded large parts of low lying farmland. In those boggy wetlands the Germans could not move their tanks so quickly. Hitler must have cursed for a while because it was not going as fast as he had wanted.

On Pentecost, a religious holiday in Holland, at noon, the German commander for the invasion forces in Holland sent an ultimatum: 'Surrender or Rotterdam will be bombed.' The Dutch ignored the ultimatum and the enemy started to bomb the town. Wave after wave of German planes dropped bombs into the heart of the city. When they were done the whole center of Rotterdam was in ruins and on fire. Hundreds of civilians were burned alive. That afternoon, we did not see one enemy plane and we were astonished that it could be so quiet. The weather was still beautiful, but we could not figure out why there was a huge cloud, blacker than black, hanging to the south of us, and we were wondering what it might be. We did not like the unusual quietness and thought that the Germans had bombed the oil installations outside Rotterdam. That's what the big fat, dark cloud would be, we thought.

It must have been around 3.30 or 4 o'clock when some people on bicycles came through the main highway that ran between Rotterdam and The Hague, screaming: "Help us, help us! Our town is on fire! The Germans have bombed everything! There are so many dead and hundreds have no homes. We are from Rotterdam! Where do we go?"

We did not know exactly what was going on, but we knew in our hearts that something terrible had happened. The Germans called it the 'Capture of Rotterdam' and we called it the 'Murder of Rotterdam', just like what they had done in Warsaw. The bombers of civilians moved in our direction and started to occupy

The Netherlands. Refugees were shoved aside so the German tanks could move to Amsterdam, the capital of the country. We did not go to the main highway to see the enemy coming. In The Hague, we let the mass murderers go north and we did not want to see them. We had to face the fact that we were beaten and that the Germans would enter our part of the country. We too would be occupied. We saw many people cry and it was one of our saddest days in the war. We had not seen a German yet and it was as if we were like a ship without a rudder.

In Belgium they were still fighting. Some of our Dutch forces had retreated to the southwest and were fighting side by side with the French in Zeeland. We felt the action would not be over for a while, but it would not be long before the gray bandits would be here and we knew very well that then the real troubles would start: no more freedom!

We heard that the Dutch government and the Dutch royal family had escaped to England to continue the war in exile. We felt lost, completely lost and very much alone. No government. No royal family. Nothing. We were alone with only bombed-out cities, blown-up bridges and destruction. We felt sad and many people openly cried.

The evening came and there was no news on the radio, just nice music to cheer us up. When we wanted to listen to the BBC, they did not have any news either. There were no more raids, so we went to bed on time.

My brother Piet and I had always done things together: bicycling, camping - we were both in the Boy Scouts and many more things - always together. When we got up the next morning, we had our breakfast and decided to go to our military airport Ypenburg, just to see what was left. We had seen it bombed from our house when the Luftwaffe tried to capture it. It was only two kilometers from our house, but we had to take a detour because there was a canal between us and the airfield.

Once we were there, we saw what a mess it was. There were German planes all over. We counted one hundred and thirty-four and according to the German reports, they had lost only four! There we saw our first Germans trying to clean up the wrecked planes that had tried to land on the main road. What a terrible sight it was!

These were the murderers who had attacked us and bombed us! What evil had we done against Germany, to be treated like this? There they were – the 'super race'! Later, when we saw them standing on top of their tanks, every German that passed by was cursed to death. We pretended not to see them. We knew that here were the murderers of civilians, the enemy, hated by many nations. Of course we could not say a thing and then we realized that our freedom was over. You could not say whatever you were thinking. You had to be quiet. But deep in our hearts we knew we would survive! Our day would come when we would get rid of this European pest.

At the time, however, we were depressed and sad. For now it was hopeless and we had to accept it.

Hundreds of refugees from Rotterdam were coming toward us from the south. We saw them coming: people who had lost everything; relatives, homes, children and everything else. They were pushed aside by German troops who were standing on top of their cars as masters and conquerors

We tried to help the refugees with clothing, bedding, pots and pans and whatever else we could spare. Many were looking for their relatives and that was a sad thing. How these poor people got to us, we will never know. The Hague was the first big town to help the refugees.

I was proud to be Dutch and everyone helped each other. Only a few traitors stood there and gave the 'Heil Hitler!' salute. How could anybody do that? It was beyond me. Some Germans were there, already giving orders. It made us feel sick to our stomachs and we swore in our hearts that our day would come. Slaves? Never!

The Germans moved in and more came. They started to occupy every town. They were in a rush to seize our capital, Amsterdam, and the mouse gray hordes moved north. We went home, we had seen enough. Now Dad had come home. We were in the living room and Mom and Dad were there and gave us a lecture, saying that we should obey the Germans. Whatever might happen, being openly against Germany would not serve our cause for freedom. They would pick you up, put you in jail and you could not do much.

There was a Jewish family living on our street. We had not known they were Jewish, but later on, when we had been occupied for months, they told us. They had seven kids and wanted to go to England, but they did not have enough money. The mother was completely out of her mind from fear! The neighbors told them they did not have to worry, that everyone in the block would take a kid. I am glad to say that they all survived the war.

The 'super race' moved in and began to occupy the Netherlands, and from that time on our troubles started. It went slowly, but we saw the first announcements and orders posted on walls and billboards. I knew I would have to go back to school. In less than two months I would have to do my final exams. That was as far into the future as I could think. Beyond that, it was too dreadful to imagine.

Probably the last taxi

Johanna Prior Bruinhout

I lived in Rotterdam. On May 9, 1940 my mother took me to see a movie for the first time in my life as a reward for passing my swimming test. That night I was a very happy young girl of thirteen. The next morning my world fell apart.

I lived with my parents behind their cigar store and near their factory on Kruis Quay, a street in the center of Rotterdam. We stayed home for three days, but then my father decided to leave, if possible, because the planes coming over flew so low that you could see the pilots.

The driver of an empty taxi, probably the last one, was willing to take us, as long as we could jump in and go straight away. He took us to a friend of my father, who had a Ffyffes banana truck and he drove us to an uncle in Schiebroek, on the northern outskirts of the city. We were there in the hallway with pans on our head on the fourteenth while our house and business were being destroyed by the bombs falling on Rotterdam. Because of a silly conflict over our dog and my uncle's cats we could not stay. So we were on the go again. My parents could stay with my mother's sister and I was farmed out to my father's sister. It took almost a year before we got an apartment together again. Then shortly afterward my mother passed away.

I cried like a small child

Dolf Hantelmann

On the day of the bombing of Rotterdam I was seventeen years old and working in the Main Post Office building as a volunteer fire guard. There were also soldiers in the building, who went into the air raid shelters when the sirens sounded. Although I initially stayed at my post and did my rounds in the building, as I felt was my duty, I too entered the shelter when the bomb-impacts increased in number.

The building started to sway and shake and the lights went out when one of the wings of the building received a direct hit.

When it became quieter we went outside. At the back of the building a soldier more or less coerced me into drinking a shot of liquor. I almost choked on it, because I had never drunk alcohol before. He probably did this to help us face what we would encounter outside. The scene was indeed horrific. Casualties lay strewn about. I saw rubble, broken windows and fire in many places. I then went to The Oppert, a nearby street, where fires were raging and we helped people climb out of basements through tiny windows. They could not leave the buildings by the regular routes.

Once I got home, it seemed as if all my pent up feelings came out. I cried for hours like a small child.

The sewing machine

Johanna Hoogeveen-van Gelderen

I lived in a second floor apartment in Kralingen, a district of Rotterdam. An incendiary bomb hit the back of our building and it burned down. My father and our neighbor, Willem Zwart, entered the building when only the roof was burning. They started in Willem's third floor apartment and threw clothing and bedding out of a window onto the street below.

When it became too hot up there they descended to the second floor and did the same thing in our apartment. At Willem's urging my dad, at the very last minute, took our sewing machine with him, because it might come in handy later, as Willem said.

Our family consisted of three people, my mother, my father and I, Jo (Johanna). We were now homeless. The afternoon of the bombing we fled to 'De Kralingse Plas', a lake in a nearby park. That night we slept in a house outside of the bombed area with other neighbors. When I remarked just after midnight: "Now it is my birthday" some of the women within hearing distance wailed. I wondered what was wrong about what I had just said. As a young ten year old girl I could not imagine the anguish that my parents and everybody else suffered.

From then on for ten long years our family lived at a number of different addresses, always staying with other people. After ten years of being homeless my parents finally moved into their own house again in the spring of 1950, five years after the end of the war.

The sewing machine that my father salvaged from the

burning house, a hand cranked machine, was indeed useful during the war years, when everything had to be mended and re-used. After the war it was also used to sew my wedding dress and later the baptismal dress, which was used for our three daughters' baptisms and also for most of our grandchildren. The sewing machine is the only item that survived the destruction. It was among my parents' household effects. They had been married for fifteen years when the bombs were dropped on our house. In the spring of 1984 we brought the machine over to Canada as excess baggage, purely for its sentimental value.

When we saw the attack on the World Trade Centre in New York we were reminded of the bombing of Rotterdam. After all those years not many people know about it anymore. It was followed by the occupation, which lasted for five years and worse events were to follow throughout The Netherlands.

The bombing did have tremendous consequences, however. A total of 84 Heinkel bombers dropped 97 tons of explosives and hundreds, if not thousands, of incendiary bombs on the city center. The onslaught lasted for about 10 minutes. The fire completely destroyed about 600 acres, and burned for 40 days and 40 nights. It destroyed 24,978 homes, 2,393 stores, 1,483 offices, 1,212 factories and workshops, 526 bars and restaurants, 256 boarding houses and lodgings, 184 garages, 69 schools, 26 hotels, 21 churches, 12 cinemas, 4 hospitals, 4 railway stations, 2 theatres and 2 museums.

Eighty thousand people became homeless, 874 people died and several hundreds were maimed for life.

The rubble had to be cleared before one could think about rebuilding. Because of the destruction of so many factories and other places of work thousands of men lost their jobs. An army of rubble clearers was formed from among these unemployed, who were supplemented with volunteers. About 20,000 men worked in the rubble itself, in other work associated with the clearing another 10,000 were active.

Many men, my father included, were compelled to work there in order to earn wages. Soon after the bombing the still smoldering ruins were torn down. This rubble was cleared with the help of a fleet of 1400 trucks. An estimated amount of 175 million cubic feet of rubble and 5,000 tons of iron were cleared in the years after the bombing. The rubble would have been sufficient to build a wall 45 miles long, 25 feet wide and 33 feet high. The iron would have sufficed to build two 30,000 ton ships.

The rubble was dumped at special sites. These sites quickly proved to be too small and the City Yards had trouble finding places where it could be dumped. A rash decision was made and several historic canals, including one called 'the Schie' were filled. From this the following saying sprung: 'Before the war the Schie was in Rotterdam, but after the war Rotterdam was in the Schie.' When even this proved insufficient a recently dug harbor was filled again with rubble.

About 25 million bricks were scraped clean and these bricks were used to build the sidewalls of the River Rotte, which had to be diverted, because of the filling of the canals.

Soon the first emergency stores were built at various points and in some of the suburbs houses were erected. After a year this activity had already slowed down because of the scarcity of materials and soon no construction took place at all. When the rubble was cleared a large open area remained in the heart of the city with only an occasional building standing here and there.

The victims of the bombing had to fend for themselves, because assistance was minimal. Most insurance policies did not cover war-related damage. Some organizations to provide assistance were formed almost immediately and the city administration provided loans in the worst cases. Help also came from the rest of the country in the form of household furniture, bedding and money. For a few months, until the end of June of 1940 emergency kitchens were operated and 35,000 people benefited from this each day, while it lasted.

Those who lived through this disaster and those who witnessed it will never forget it.

Left-over lunch

Coby Markwat

I will never forget May 14, 1940. I was nine years old and lived in Rotterdam. Dad, mom, my two sisters and I were sitting at the table for our midday meal. I can still see my Mom standing in front of the window and saying to my dad: "Jan, come have a look at what is falling out of the sky." As soon as she spoke those words all hell broke loose. The noise was deafening, the ground was shaking and we all huddled under the stairs. It seemed to go on for hours, even though in reality it was only about ten minutes. We heard glass breaking and neighbors screaming.

When finally the bombs stopped falling we saw our upstairs neighbors. They were also eating when it all happened and for protection they had put pots on their heads. Their shoulders were covered with left-over lunch! Funny, the things you remember!

After the all-clear signal, dad opened the front door and we saw that the sky was covered in thick smoke. There was a horrible burning smell. This smell would hang over the city for months, making it hard to breathe. We were lucky, our street was not bombed, but on the corner there was a Jewish Hospital, which had received a direct hit. When we got outside we saw an arm lying in the gutter and our parents pulled us back into the house. This sight and the smell of the city burning stayed with me my whole life.

Most of central Rotterdam was gone, or still burning and everybody tried to find their relatives. Here we were lucky again, grandma, grandpa and the rest of the family were safe.

On this horrible day, our Uncle Karel jumped on his motorbike to go and find his two daughters, Bep and Tinie, who were staying in a Catholic orphanage in the center of Rotterdam. He drove through burning streets and when he arrived at the orphanage it was engulfed in flames. Uncle Karel was desperate and ran around the burning building. At one spot he heard a humming noise, like bees in a beehive. He found a cellar door where the noise was very loud. He threw himself against the door, but discovered that it was barricaded from the inside. Suddenly he knew what the humming noise was! It was the kids saying Hail Marys. When the children realized there was help, they screamed and cried. Finally the door opened and Karel led the nuns and children outside. The fire around the building was so severe that the veils of the nuns caught fire. Karel had the children make a chain and made them cover their mouths. He guided 71 kids to safety through a burning city. In the evening two pale brave girls (our nieces) were dropped off at our place and they stayed with us for a while.

After a week people started to clear the ruins and began building temporary wooden stores. The strength of people to survive and to rebuild a city from the ashes is amazing.

Legs like rubber

Anne Kluver

I was born in Rotterdam and was eighteen years old when the war broke out in 1939. Holland was invaded the following year in May of 1940, just before my nineteenth birthday. I lived in the centre of the city near Wester Singel during the bombing of Rotterdam and until the liberation of Holland in May of 1945.

On May 10 we heard that German paratroopers had landed near the bridges over the Maas river. Their objective, of course, was the harbor which was and still is the largest in Europe. At that time, we were so naive and unaware of the consequences of war that my boyfriend, who lived in the northern part of Rotterdam, stood with his dad and two brothers on the rooftop of their house watching the German paratroopers land. They could easily have been killed by the bullets that were flying. The fighting between the Dutch troops and the Germans was heavy and there were many casualties on both sides. I think that the Germans were quite surprised to find so much resistance.

The fighting continued for the next three days, during which the citizens of Rotterdam tried to be brave and did their best to ensure that life remained as normal as possible under the circumstances. I went to my job as a store clerk in the west end of the city as usual. During that time, we heard horrible stories about Jewish people taking their own lives. People were terrified and were afraid to go to sleep.

On May 14 I was in the store with a colleague. My

boyfriend had come to help us and give us moral support. He had been unable to go to his place of work, because it was in the area where all the fighting was taking place. It was about 10 o'clock in the morning when the alarm sounded and that meant we had to go to the air raid shelter, which was right across from our store in a small park. The shelter was packed with people all scared to death. Children were crying and some people were praying as we could feel the ground shaking when the bombs fell.

Nothing prepared us for what we saw when we came out of the shelter. A big black cloud of smoke hung over the entire city, but it was thickest over the city centre. My boyfriend and I decided to walk towards my home (a walk of about 30 to 45 minutes). I'll never forget the feeling of terror that I experienced as we got closer to my house. My legs felt like rubber and I was certain that I was the only survivor in our entire family.

We saw that half of Rotterdam was ablaze - a sight I will never forget. To my relief, I found my parents, three sisters and one of my two brothers standing outside of our home, dirty from falling ashes but alive. My other brother returned later and had his own horror stories to tell. Our house was saved because a wide canal that ran behind our neighborhood prevented the fire from crossing.

I remember that they were trying to rescue people hanging onto a cable on the other side of the canal. Hundreds of people were killed by the bombs or perished in the flames. We were not allowed back in our house, but were evacuated for several days before we could go back to sleep in our own beds again, exhausted but happy to be alive! Little did we know that this was the beginning of five years of fear, oppression, hunger and cold, which ended when we were very thankfully liberated by Canadian, American and British troops in May of 1945.

We survived the war and my boyfriend became my husband. We had two children and the four of us immigrated to Canada in 1953 settling in the Ottawa area, where we have lived ever since. My husband and I were happily married for 58 years until his death in 2002.

Rotterdam was rebuilt and is now one of the most modern cities in Europe.

The last bananas

Josine Eikelenboom

I t was a beautiful morning in the month of May. In Rotterdam our whole family: parents, sister, brother and I, stood on the sidewalk in front of our house among a group of neighbors. We stared into the pale blue sky, where high above us flew, like just so many starlings, swarms of airplanes. I was four years old and the word that I heard over and over was etched into my memory: "Invasion! Invasion!" That day the German bombs only fell on the harbor. But immediately the food supply became chaotic. Everyone tried to stockpile what they could get their hands on. A tradesman pushed a handcart loaded with bananas down our street. Those were the last bananas that I would see for many years.

A few days later the bombs fell on our city's downtown core. Our refuge was in the rest room underneath the stairs, which had to protect us from falling beams. Everyone had to put a pot on their heads, against shards of glass and shrapnel. Our maid, Sjaan, got the colander. Suddenly the bombs started falling really close by, I can still see the wall of the rest room swaying back and forth. But our house was spared.

My father was an air raid 'block warden' for our street. He went outside wearing a scary looking gas mask. The house on the corner, with three apartments in it, had been transformed into a pile of rubble. I remember a crying Mr. Voogt, sitting in our hallway, a glass of water in his shaking hand. My mother whispered to us that his wife had been killed and that his daughter had lost both her legs. The city was in ruins and fires burned everywhere.

A large washtub
with drinking water

Joe van Dyke

I was eleven years old in May 1940 when a cruel enemy attacked our peaceful country. The impressions of the five days of war are vividly imprinted on my mind. The second day of the war, when the schools were closed, I played a game of soccer with some other boys in the street where we lived, a few blocks from the center of Rotterdam. All of a sudden we heard a terrific whistling sound and a tremendous explosion. A German airplane had dropped a bomb a couple of streets behind us. The impact created a massive cloud of dust, enveloping us, so that we could not see anything. I lost all sense of direction until the dust settled a little and I could grope my way to the front door of our house. That was a very scary experience.

Later that day we saw a Dutch Air Force plane on fire being chased by a German fighter, very low over the rooftops of the homes across the street from us. We never found out what happened to the Dutch pilot.

Then on May 14 we were alarmed by the sound of many German bombers flying overhead. We saw them dive, bombing the center of Rotterdam, destroying its very heart, and killing many innocent civilians, even damaging the hospital on Cool Singel, a major downtown street.

Billows of smoke and flames drifted over the city. Frustrated and helpless, Dutch soldiers stood on our street corner firing their rifles at the aircraft overhead, without inflicting any damage as far as we could see. How can one ever forget the stream of refugees fleeing the danger as they came through our street with whatever belongings they could carry on carts and bikes, many with infants and babies in their arms. No one knew where to go. One man walked past us with butter running out of his pocket. Some were injured and bleeding, many were upset and distraught.

Our parents had filled a large washtub with drinking water as a precaution, in the case the public utilities would get cut off. But the water was rendered undrinkable, because of the ashes and debris from the bombing and the ensuing fires.

The Dutch Army capitulated to prevent further casualties and the destruction of other cities. So began the occupation of The Netherlands. Our lives would never be the same and the events of World War II still affect us, even after all these years.

We gave them fresh tomatoes

Dirk Hoogeveen

Tuesday May 14th, 1940 was a beautiful warm spring day. It was just after Pentecost and it was the fifth day after the invasion by the Germans. In the early afternoon Rotterdam was bombed by the German Air Force with devastating effects. For the population this bombing came like a lightning bolt out of a blue sky. From Bleiswijk, where I lived, the circling airplanes were clearly visible and we could hear their drone as well as the explosions of the bombs. Smoke spread over the city as the fires spread. The cloud of smoke and flames rose higher and higher into the sky. It is difficult to describe such an enormous fire. It raged for many days, the sun disappeared and became an orange globe and the stench of the fire was overpowering. Ash rained down until the inferno was well past its height. Because the main water pipeline was hit by bombs the Rotterdam Fire Department was powerless and hence the resulting damage was enormous.

Within an hour after the bombing a great stream of dazed fleeing people appeared in Bleiswijk, just north of Rotterdam. The only thing that we could do was offer them a glass of water, because our town had its own water supply, and fresh tomatoes from the hothouses near the town. We did this for hours on end. Most of the fleeing people had lost all of their possessions and were desperate. Some were still running. From where they ran they knew, but they had no idea where they were going to.

At that time I went to school in Hilligersberg, a suburb of Rotterdam and a few weeks after the bombing our school reopened, but in subsequent years going to school in a normal way did not happen again. As the school itself was occupied by German troops and used as barracks, the classes were divided over a number of other buildings, including a church.

In the summer of 1940 I often wandered in the cheerless debris of a once proud city, a pitiful ruin of bricks and misery.

German blood

Bouk Jobsis

The tenth of May was such an enticing, sunny day. In the freshness of morning flowers and trees blooming, birds singing, the sky was a clear blue. I lived on the outskirts of Leeuwarden on a little side road with five detached houses with meadows in front and behind and farms and market gardens close by. How I loved our own garden, with lots of plants and even some berry bushes. My girlfriend from next door and I walked to school as we always did and we took such pleasure in our well-known and well-loved world. School was dismissed.

The next day a friend and I, both nine years old, followed other people to Groningen Road which leads into the city from the east. There we saw an astonishing sight: marching soldiers in grey uniforms and shiny black boots waving, laughing and singing. We also saw tanks and trucks. We, the Dutch, mostly women and children – the men were still at work – watched in eerie silence. Some women had tears streaming down their cheeks.

A few days later we were told that Rotterdam had been bombed. The country had surrendered to the Germans and the queen had fled to England. We knew our safe little world had changed and we did not yet understand what it all would mean. I for one was very ill-informed, we did not even have a radio at home. Had we not been neutral during World War I?

Our national anthem played through my head. It is

called 'William of Nassau'. William was the leader of the Dutch resistance against Spanish oppression in the 16th century and the anthem is written as if it is sung by him. He was born in Dillenburg in Germany.

The first verse starts with the words: 'William of Nassau, I am of German blood.' As those words played through my head I thought: 'we have German in our blood?'

Burnt documents

Ann Hendren

I n August of 1939 dad was called up by the military, put in a uniform and was stationed in a makeshift hospital set up in a castle about 40 miles from home. He was placed in a surgical unit specializing in lower jaw surgery.

I will never forget the smoke and ashes that floated over Utrecht, where we lived, from Rotterdam, which is 30 miles from Utrecht. We could hardly breathe and large pieces of burnt documents fluttered down into our street.

German troops soon arrived, marching into our country. It was the start of an unspeakable horror which came as such a contrast to the beautiful warm sunny spring filled with blossoming trees, and blooming tulips and narcissus everywhere. My twelve year old heart was filled with fear and uncertainty about the future. The five days of heavy fighting had a great impact on me. Once the capitulation was announced, I slept for 12 solid hours until I was awoken by the German tanks rolling by on Leiden Road. Those images made such an impact that I have never forgotten them. We did not know it yet, but there would be five years of misery, fear, and hunger before the war would end.

The gravel flew off the roof

Jantina Smittenaar

On May 10, 1940 we lived in The Hague, I was eight years old. The houses in our street had flat roofs with gravel on them. On that terrible day I heard planes flying over. The sound was so loud I thought for sure they would fly into the house. I looked out of the window and could see the pilot inside the plane and the gravel was flying off the roof into the street. It was really scary.

Something else I saw when looking out of the window was soldiers on each corner of the street with their guns ready to shoot. Ours was a very short block and all four corners had soldiers.

When looking out the window four days later, we saw that the sky was red. Rotterdam was on fire. We were done fighting. That is, done fighting out in the open. Everyone knows the fighting really went on for another five years.

A jar of cherry jam

Nan Casey

I was just 17 years old and lived in Zeist. I had started working in Utrecht as a telephone operator for the national telephone company, PTT. I lived at home with my parents and a sister who was two years older than I. My father had a store on the town's main street, where a streetcar passed every half hour or so. I travelled to Utrecht for my work and with the split shifts that I worked I spent a lot of time on that tram.

The morning of May 10 we woke early because planes were passing over low. Our windows were open. We ran outside in our night clothes and we saw German planes with swastikas on their wings. Of course we knew about the other countries that had been overrun. We had heard Hitler scream on the radio and in the cinema newsreels. But we believed Holland would escape the fate of the other countries. We had been neutral in World War I, so we hoped it would be the same this time.

Nobody knew what to do, so I simply went to Utrecht on the streetcar, to go to work. When I got there, they sent me back because I was so young. They told me I could have my job back after the fighting was over.

I was at home during those terrible first days of the war. Nobody knew what you were supposed to be doing. The store was open, everybody was out in the street with the radio on. We heard about paratroopers coming down disguised as civilians and even as priests, but not in Zeist. The soldiers that had been billeted in Zeist had all gone to their stations or wherever, we did not know where. One part of Zeist had to be evacuated to another part of the town, so I helped evacuate a nursing home to keep busy, pushing a handcart across town.

Then on the third day, a group of soldiers arrived by train at the station in Zeist. They had been at the Grebbe Line. They sat down on the steps to the station, very depressed, and we tried to help.

We heard on the radio that Queen Wilhelmina and the Dutch government had gone to England. We heard about Rotterdam being bombed so terribly and also that if Holland did not capitulate Utrecht would be bombed like Rotterdam.

We had our first air raid alarm. Everybody had to go inside. Doors were locked, blinds pulled down. My mother gave us a spoonful of medicine for our nerves. Someone banged on the door of the store and my dad opened up. The newlywed couple, who owned the cigar shop next door, came in. My mother gave them a spoonful of medicine too. The young woman was scared to be alone with her husband, so they stayed with us during the alarm. Then someone else rang the doorbell. It was an old man who wanted to buy a jar of cherry jam. My dad thought that was an excuse and that he just wanted to come in because he was afraid too. But the man said: "What are you afraid of? I just want the jam and go home. I am not afraid of bombs and bullets". He had fought in the Dutch East Indies and had seen war before. So we just started laughing as a nervous reaction, until we cried. Fortunately no planes came and no bombs fell. Our neighbors went home when the safety signal sounded. No more nerves, but we did wonder what would happen the next day.

Well, the next day I went back to Utrecht to work. The

Germans troops marched in on the highway into Utrecht, ten abreast in full battle dress, singing. Everybody on the main road had to watch that. It was terrible to see!

Steps of hope

Paulina Rompelman

While watching the Cenotaph Service recently, I suddenly remembered vividly one of the experiences of my youth. Not that the incident I remembered took place on a bleak November day. On the contrary, it started in May and it lasted for five years. And if 'incident' is not the right word for a five year period, neither is 'remembering' exactly the right word for the sensation I felt that recent Remembrance Day. It is more appropriate to describe it as the surfacing of facts, hidden deep in my subconscious, that were instrumental in shaping my whole outlook on life.

As I said, it started in the early spring of the year in which I would turn ten years old. My mother, three year old brother Casey and I, Leena, had temporarily moved from The Hague, where I was born, to a small village in the eastern part of Holland where my stepfather Casey Senior was stationed as a soldier in the Dutch Army. My mother Connie was the clingy type and had followed him there because she was afraid he would go astray. As innocent children we did not realize that our country, or actually the whole of Europe, was threatened by a very ugly and all-encompassing war and that mobilization of the Dutch Army was already in progress. Oblivious to the rumblings in the world around us, little Casey and I were delighted with the activity on the large pig farm where we stayed. It was operated by an older couple.

Time and again little Casey and I were fascinated as we watched the chickens balancing themselves on the pigs' backs and saw them bob their little beaks in swift but graceful movements to pick unsuspecting bugs from between the stubble on their hosts' hides. And it was an exciting experience for us city folks to be awakened in the middle of the night by shouts that the ice in the nearby river was shifting and threatened to inundate its bordering 'polders', so that every able man was required to help sandbag the dikes. In the beginning of May, when the weather turned warmer, Casey and I went exploring the meadows around the farm, picking snowbells and enjoying the sun, which was steadily increasing in strength.

One night my parents went to a barn dance and I was allowed to go with them to watch, while the old farmer and his wife baby-sat little Casey. We returned home late. This was the first time in my young life that I was up so late and I remember that I hopped and skipped the whole way back to the farm. The spring night was full of promise of approaching summer and the sky was bright with blinking stars. We went to bed, but our peace and quiet was brutally shattered at around 3.30 a.m. when we were awakened by the drone of huge numbers of airplanes.

Around dawn we could see that the sky was full of them and we also noticed some parachutes like miniature ice cream umbrellas descending amidst small puffs of smoke. The ill-prepared Dutch Army had recovered somewhat from their rude awakening and attempted to parry the German attack with anti-aircraft artillery. My stepfather jumped on his bicycle to travel the short distance to the local Army Headquarters where he had to report, while my mother and I fearfully waved goodbye to him from the kitchen door. Looking up we saw a crippled German plane whose pilot decided to jettison his remaining bombs and just before we ran back into the house to hide under the big kitchen table (a lot of good that would have done...), we witnessed the incredible sight of the bombs buzzing down like giant hissing cigars. They hit the ground with ear-shattering thuds and sand, gravel and grass mushroomed up in the air, completely hiding from view the little speck on the road that big Casey had become by that time.

For hour after torturing hour we did not know for sure what had happened to him. Fortunately, when he finally came back home it turned out that he was neither hit nor hurt. He had looked back over his shoulder and had seen the incendiary bombs coming down. He had pedaled like crazy to get out of their almost predictable path.

Women and children had to be removed from the war zone so my mother, little Casey and I were evacuated from place to place, sleeping in trucks, barracks and closed factories until we arrived in a little village, Zoetermeer, close to our home town of The Hague. The day we arrived there we saw the brutal bombing of Rotterdam. Even though Rotterdam is some twelve miles from Zoetermeer, we could quite clearly see the deadly fireworks in the sky and hear the awful sounds of the steady flow of bombs that turned the heart of the port city into a pile of rubble. The next day, while dragging ourselves and our suitcases along the only street of the village, a kind resident invited us into his home and offered some refreshments. In his house we heard with tears in our eyes and fear in our hearts and souls the radio broadcast by General Winkelman announcing the surrender of the Dutch Army to the German forces. That was the beginning of five years of Nazi occupation, a time period that is fragmentally embedded in my memory with many bad, but strangely enough, also some good experiences.

In the beginning the German soldiers were probably told to behave kindly to the locals and they tried to win the people over with suggestions of Aryan brotherhood. I remember that there were some tanks with soldiers a couple of streets away from where we lived and curious as little girls are, I went over to see them for myself. In my ten-year old eyes the uniformed men looked handsome enough to represent the big brother I never had: "You want some chocolate, little girl, I have a little sister just like you at home!"

Although the whole matter of the occupation seemed more like a nuisance to me than a threat I noticed that the people started hoarding sugar and flour, enough for the couple of months they thought the war would last. After a little while my stepfather joined us again. The Dutch army had been disbanded and of course prohibited, but the soldiers were not yet sent to work in German factories, nor to prisoner of war camps.

But very soon after the invasion the overtures of brotherhood and togetherness between the German and Dutch people were rejected by the latter. The events on the birthday of Prince Bernhard, Princess Juliana's husband, were the turning point I have always believed. He was a German himself, but in the three years he had been married to the heir to the throne, he had already proved himself to be a true and loyal Dutchman. The Germans, of course, had denounced the members of the Royal Family who had all taken flight to England. Demonstrations of loyalty to the 'royal traitors', as the Germans called them, were strictly forbidden. As the

Prince's birthday drew near the tension mounted. You could hear people whisper about it on street corners. Flowers and fabric in the national colors, especially our precious orange, symbol of loyalty to the royal family, started to disappear from the stores. But still the Germans did not suspect nor expect what was happening. They did not put any extra sentries on duty at strategic points, so they were not prepared when on Saturday June 29, in the early morning hours, the steps of the royal palace in the heart of The Hague were stealthily covered with a variety of red, white and blue, but mostly orange flowers. It was a silent expression of rejection of the occupational forces as well as a threat of rebellion. The old guards opened the doors to the palace and everybody who wished to could sign the Prince's birthday book. Even the staunchest socialist was an eager royalist on that day! When they ran out of paper, the people just used blank sheets of paper - even toilet paper - to sign their names.

Of course when the Germans caught on they closed off the streets leading to the palace and had the flowers removed. But still I am convinced that they understood the hidden message that although the occupation was a fact, the true free spirit of the Hollanders could not be broken. It made them realize, I think, that they might have scored a victory in battle, but were already beginning to lose the war against the stubborn resolve of united citizens, an underground rebellion that would last almost five years. Yes, on that beautiful summer day in June of 1940, the flowers on the steps of the deserted palace instilled an unspoken message of strength and hope in the people of Holland, a message to withstand whatever was coming to them!

Contributors

Harm Duursma
Harm was born in Groningen in 1915. He moved to Hengelo in 1937 and emigrated to Canada in 1953. He currently resides in White Rock, British Columbia.

Lisette de Groot
Lisette was born in the Dutch East Indies. When she was three years old her mother died and she went to stay with an aunt and uncle in Rotterdam for two and a half years. Her father remarried and the family lived in Voorschoten when the war started. Lisette and her husband emigrated to Jacksonville, Florida in 1964 to work at the American office of a Dutch Company. They retired to Asheville, North Carolina, where they still live.

Caty de Graaf
Caty was born in Utrecht and turned six on the day of the German invasion in 1940. She immigrated to California in 1962 with her husband and four year old daughter. Not having completed her formal education in The Netherlands, she went to night school in the USA, now as a single mom of two, to get her high school diploma. She graduated in 1987. In 1995 she moved to Michigan to be close to her daughter and grandchildren. She lives in Marine City, Michigan.

Riekje Brandsma
Riekje Brandsma grew up in Friesland, where her father owned a shipyard. She was the eldest of six children

and celebrated her 21st birthday on an immigrant ship on the Atlantic, coming to Canada in 1954. She settled in the Cornwall, Ontario area. Eventually most of the family returned to The Netherlands, but Riekje and one of her brothers stayed in Canada.

Maria Neijmeijer
Maria Neijmeijer grew up in Abcoude and emigrated to Canada in 1958. She first settled in Saskatchewan, but spent thirty years on Vancouver Island near Victoria, with her husband and her four children. When they retired Maria and her husband returned to Saskatchewan, where they still live in Saskatoon.

Gerrit Top
Gerrit lives in High River, Alberta.

Peter Verhesen
Peter Verhesen was ten years old when the war started in 1940. He emigrated to Canada in 1954, married in Oosterwierum in 1956 and raised a family of three in Fort Smith, North West Territories and Trochu, Alberta.

Susan Rombeek
Susan was born and raised in The Hague and emigrated to Seattle with her husband in 1957. She now lives on Guemes Island in Washington State.

Jerry Meents
Jerry was nine years old when the Germans invaded Holland. Jerry's father was Jewish, his mother was not. The family lived in Amsterdam in the Transvaal-neighborhood, which had a large Jewish population. He

fought in the Israeli war of independence in 1948/49, but returned to Amsterdam afterward. In 1957 he came to the USA with his wife, his seven year old son and $1.25 in his pocket. He settled in Ogden, Utah, where he still lives.

Roland Krijgsman

Roland Krijgsman was born in Middelharnis. He was twelve years old when the war started. He emigrated to the USA in 1955 with his wife. They settled in Clifton, New Jersey, where they still live. In October of 2010 Roland published his autobiography, covering the war years and his life up to immigration to the USA. It is called 'A Boy from Flakkee'.

John Keulen

John was born near Chicago in 1931 to Dutch immigrant parents. They returned to The Netherlands when John was two years old and settled in the Frisian village of Bakhuizen. John's parents emigrated to the United States for a second time after the war, in 1948, accompanied by John, then seventeen and his brother. John lives in Port Orange, Florida.

John Vandermeer

John was born in the Dutch East Indies in 1930 and moved to The Netherlands when he was one year old. He lived in Groningen with his parents when the war broke out. John got married to his wife, Johanna, in 1951. In 1954 they emigrated to Canada together, where they lived in Toronto for 16 years before moving to British Columbia. John and Johanna now live in Nanaimo, British Columbia. In 2010 John received a medal of recognition for living with diabetes for 50 years, Johanna received a certificate of recognition for her support and dedication. John's diabetes was likely caused by deprivation suffered during the last year of the war.

Ernest Meershoek and Adriana Meershoek-Dekker

Ernest was born in The Hague and Adriana in the village of Etten. They met when Ernest came to Etten after the war to regain his strength. In 1957 Ernest moved to Canada and in 1959 Adriana followed him. They got married in Toronto. Adriana worked as a dental assistant and Ernest worked in the movie industry. They are now retired and they still live in Toronto.

Christina Dodenbier

Christina was born in Amsterdam, but lived in Ede when the war started. She was eleven years old. In 1951 she followed her fiancé to Salt Lake City, where they initially settled. Later she moved to Ogden, where she still lives.

Jacoba Robertson

Jacoba lives in Bramalea, Ontario.

Gerty Heinen

Gerty was born shortly after the war in Bunschoten-Spakenburg. She came to Canada in 1955 at the age of six. Her family settled in Alberta, where she still lives. Gerty was an elementary school teacher for 33 years. She wrote down the stories her parents told her.

Willy Mensing Traa

Willy was born in the village of Achterveld. She was five

years old when war broke out. When she was seventeen she came to Canada with her mother, her father and nine brothers and sisters. The family settled in Winnipeg, where Willy still lives with her husband.

Jack de Pagter

Jack was seventeen years old when the war started. To avoid being sent to Germany for forced labor he escaped through Belgium into France, where the resistance helped him hide. He joined the US Army when they liberated France and he fought in France, Holland, Germany and Austria. In 1949 he moved to Aspen, Colorado, where he ran a ski lodge until his recent retirement.

He wrote a book about his experiences called 'Destination Aspen', from which his contribution to this volume is an adapted excerpt.

Johanna Prior Bruinhout

Johanna was born in Rotterdam. She was thirteen years old when the war started. After liberation she joined the Dutch Navy. She was sent to the Dutch East Indies, where she was stationed during the Indonesian War of Independence from 1947 until 1950. In 1950 she got a job in Paris, where she met het husband. Together they emigrated to Canada in 1952, where they lived in Montreal for thirteen years, before moving to the United States. Johanna now lives in Davie, Florida.

Dolf Hantelmann

Dolf was seventeen when the war started. He worked for the Dutch postal service. He emigrated to Canada in 1963, where he started his own business as a piano tuner in Edmonton, Alberta. For 25 years he presented a

Dutch language radio program for CKER in Edmonton, where he still lives.

Johanna Hoogeveen-van Gelderen
Johanna van Gelderen turned 10 years old on the sixth day of the Second World War in Holland, May 15, 1940. She lived in Kralingen, a part of Rotterdam, with her parents when the bombing took place. Her family lost everything in the bombing and was more or less homeless for more than ten years. She married her husband Dirk in 1953, a month before coming to Canada.

Coby Markwat
Coby was born in Rotterdam and was nine years old when the city was bombed on May 14. She evacuated to Boxtel in the southern province of Brabant after the bombing, where she lived until the end of the war. After the war she moved to The Hague, where she got married in 1954. In 1956 she came to Vancouver with her husband. Together they ran a motel for many years and subsequently a bed & breakfast. Coby and her husband are retired now and live in New Westminster, near Vancouver.

Anne Kluver
Anne Kluver was eighteen years old when the war started. She lived in Rotterdam and moved to Canada in 1953, where she settled in the Ottawa area, where she still lives.

Josine Eikelenboom
Josine was born in Rotterdam and was four years old

when the war started. After the trauma of the bombing of Rotterdam, her family moved to Arnhem, where four years later she had to live through Operation Market Garden. In 1979 she came to Canada with her husband and children. She lives in Maple Ridge, British Columbia.

Joe van Dyke

Joe was 11 years old and lived in Rotterdam when the war broke out. In 1953 he moved to Canada with his wife and one year old son. The family were sent to Saskatoon, but moved to Ontario after three years. Joe and his wife now live in Clinton, Ontario.

Dirk Hoogeveen

Dirk Hoogeveen was almost 13 years old when The Netherlands were invaded by Germany. He had just started school in the Hilligersberg district of Rotterdam on March 1, 1940. His mother, who was the postmaster of Bleiswijk, was a widow with seven children. Dirk was the only boy.

Dirk came to Canada with his wife in 1953 and settled in Regina, where he worked for the Saskatchewan Power Corporation for 32 years until his retirement. Dirk has written a monthly column for De Krant, Monthly Magazine for Canadians and Americans of Dutch origin, since 1980.

Bouk Jobsis

Before coming to the United States in 1964 Bouk lived in The Netherlands, where she worked as a midwife - she delivered more than 200 babies - and Iran. She settled in Houston, Texas after a year in Utah. Bouk has two daughters.

Ann Hendren
Ann was twelve years old when the war started and lived in Utrecht. She now lives in Showlow, Arizona.

Jantina Smittenaar
Jantina was born in The Hague and was eight years old when the war started. She came to the USA in 1955, where she first spent a year in Florida, before moving to Maryland, where she currently lives.

Nan Casey
Nan Casey was seventeen years old and worked for the Dutch national telephone company when the Germans invaded. She lived in Zeist near Utrecht, where she stayed for the duration of the war. Two days after liberation in May of 1945 she met a Canadian soldier, Frank 'Red' Casey. In July they got engaged, but they had to wait until December before they were allowed to marry. Frank returned to Canada in January of 1946 and Nan followed him in September on a ship full of War Brides from all over Europe. They settled in Penticton, British Columbia, where Frank worked in the Nickel Plate gold mine. After seven years they moved to Saskatoon where Nan still lives.

Paulina Rompelman
Paulina was born in The Hague, where she lived when the war broke out. She moved to Canada in 1967, with her husband, her four year old daughter and a Siamese cat in a basket. She settled in Fredericton, New Brunswick, where she still lives.